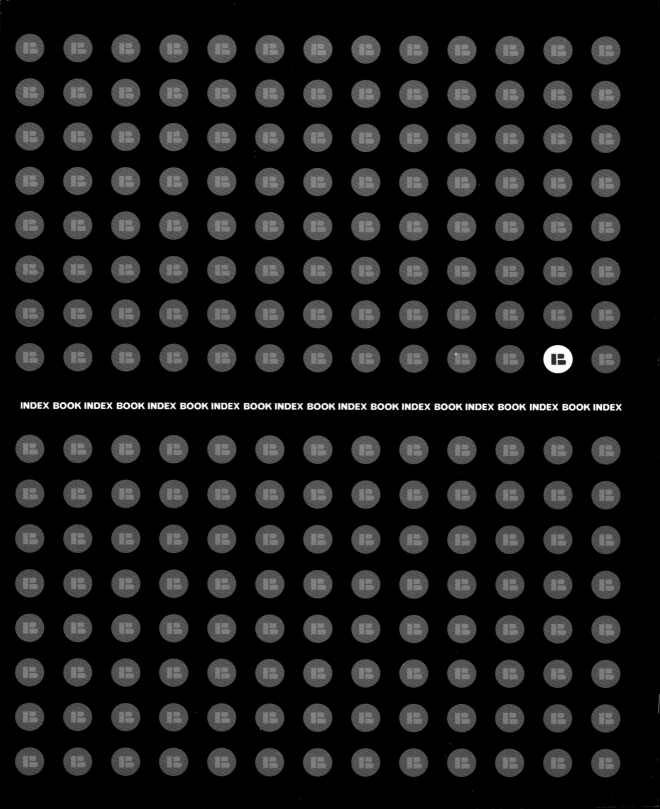

INDEX BOOK INDEX BOOK INDEX BOOK INDEX BOOK INDEX BOOK INDEX BOOK INDEX BOOK INDEX BOOK INDEX BOOK INDEX

IGNASI VICH

Ignasi Vich is a multidisciplinary designer and director of the National Visual Communication Awards, Letra Awards and of the Spanish graphic design awards, the Anuaria Awards. He has published specialty books on graphic design-related topics and a number of articles and studies in technical journals.

Together with Teresa Miret i Francesca Enrich, he was a recipient of the Gumersind Bisbal research award for the study "Pedra seca a l'Anoia" (Dry stone in Anoia).

He is a founding member of the Altamira School, a school dedicated to the art of signage.

Currently, he is promoting and participating in several architectural projects and also writes children's stories.

Publishing: INDEX BOOK ,SL
C/ Consell de Cent 160 Local 3 08015 BARCELONA
phone: *+34 93 454 55 47*
fax: *+34 93 454 84 38*
e-mail: *ib@indexbook.com*
URL: *www.indexbook.com*

Author and Art direction: *Ignasi Vich*
Design assistant: *Ester Comenge*
for any questions about Just Labels edition
e-mail: *ivich@filnet.es*

Printing: S.A de Litografía
C/ Ramón Casas, n 2 08911 BADALONA (Barcelona)
tel: *+34 93 384 76 76*
fax: *+34 464 24 51*
Contact: *Hugo Romero +34 619 752 511*
e-mail: *sa.litografia@telefonica.net*

ISBN: 978-84-96309-51-7
D.L.B.: B-49.017-2004

Printed in Spain

Dedicated to Jujú, from whom, by listening to his travels, we learn to be better people.

I would like to thank all of the designers who have collaborated on this and other projects of mine for their trust and valuable contributions, especially Ester for her dedication, patience and excitement she brought to Just Labels and the team from Index Book for once again showing faith in my work.

Thank you all.

I.V.E.

label [1275–1325. Middle English, ornamental strip of cloth, from Old French, probably of Germanic origin.] *n* **1** An item used to identify something or someone, as a small piece of paper or cloth attached to an article to designate its origin, owner, contents, use, or destination. **2** A descriptive term; an epithet. **3** A distinctive name or trademark identifying a product or manufacturer, especially a recording company. **4** Architecture A molding over a door or window; a dripstone. **5** Heraldry A figure in a field consisting of a narrow horizontal bar with several pendants. **6** Chemistry See tracer.

author [1250-1300. Middle English auctour, from Old French autor, from Latin auctor] *n* **1 a)** The writer of a book, article, or other text. **b)** One who practices writing as a profession. **2** One who writes or constructs an electronic document or system, such as a website. **3** An originator or creator, as of a theory or plan. **4** Author God.

Labels are that part of a product that heroically defends its attributes. When there isn't a container, when there is no packaging, labels are there to explain everything there is to know about a product and whether you can make it better or help make it more attractive. In this sense, labels are the great heroes of the product war, the heroes of the market.

This is my third book, or rather, this is my third compilation. The first was about signs, the second pictograms, and now it's labels. It's taken three books for me to realize that I'm not their author and that the only thing I've done is collect and select. I have been, without a doubt, a privileged reader. I've had the chance to enjoy works by real authors even before they've published their work. I've even been able to decide who makes and who doesn't. Even so, now I'm very aware of the fact that despite it all, I'm not the author. The authors are the designers who have contributed their ideas, and I offer my respect and gratitude up to each and every one of them. I've only done the work of those archivists, who, with all due rigor, classify and organize the work of artists who are the real authors of their work.

This is my most recent compilation. I sincerely hope that it is to the liking of the authors and readers who have picked it up. I thank you all for the opportunity to share in your success. Thank you all for your confidence.

SUMMARY

BODY CARE

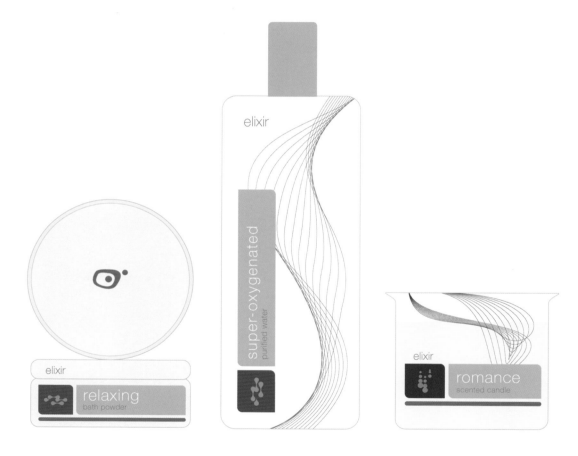

016. Elixir Spa product labels / Ida Cheinman / Adhesive / General audience

Rico en emolientes naturales
frena la pérdida de agua
y es un eficaz rehidratante

body milk

LAVANDA PUIG

017. Lavanda Puig, body milk / Isidre Barnils / Adhesive / General audience

018. Milton Baby Care / Carré Noir Barcelona / Adhesive / General audience

019. Lida / Jordi Duró Trouillet / Adhesive / General audience

020. Clenosan Gama / Carré Noir Barcelona / Adhesive / General audience

025. Frizzante / Ana Clapés / Adhesive / General audience

026. Frizzante / Ana Clapés / Others / General audience

HIDRO
GENESSE

GEL DE BAÑO
CON CREMA
HIDRATANTE

Todos los activos
+ hidra t antes
de una crema
corporal

máxima hidratación

027. Hidrogenesse, gel de baño / Isidre Barnils / Adhesive / General audience

DRINK

030. Vins Piñol: Mather Teresina Selección / Ignasi Vilà / Adhesive / General audience

031. Agua Mineral Natural Viladrau / Carol García del Busto y Pablo Merseburger / Adhesive / General audience

032. Vins Piñol: Avi Arrufí / Ignasi Vilà / Adhesive / General audience

033. Baron de Guardia / Marc Mir / Others / General audience

034. Viña María Luisa / Juanjo Lázaro Espinosa / Adhesive / General audience

035. Compass Box Whisky (see www.compassboxwhisky.com) New Yok Adhesive Labels (2) / Christopher Edmunds
/ Adhesive / General audience

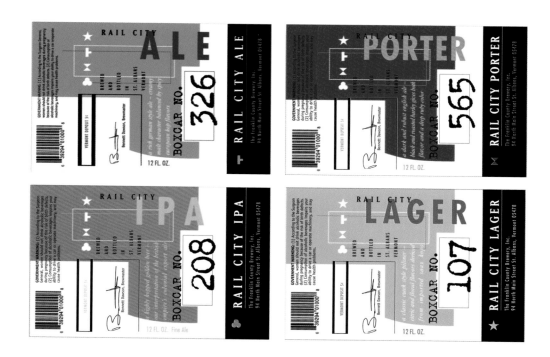

036. Rail City Brewery / Ida Cheinman / Adhesive / General audience

037. Compass Box Whisky (see www.compassboxwhisky.com) Paris Adhesive Bottle Label/ Christopher Edmunds
/ Adhesive / General audience

038. Vinho Cartuxa / Pedro Albuquerque / Adhesive / General audience

039. Saddlerock Wine, Malibu Family Wines / Brian Dolen / Adhesive / General audience

040. Vinho Cerca Nova / Pedro Albuquerque / Adhesive / General audience

045. Sammy Naranja / Juha Fiilin / Adhesive / General audience

046. Gaseosas Chap / Daniel González Ferrer / Adhesive / General audience

047. Celler Josep M. Ferret Guasch / Simbiolisi - Albert G. Burzon / Adhesive / General audience

048. Viña Lauthier / Yolanda Martin Sintes / Adhesive / General audience

reserva
BRUT NATURE

FECHA DEGÜELLE:

reserva **BRUT**

FECHA DEGÜELLE:

049. Celler Josep M. Ferret Guasch / Simbiolisi - Albert G. Burzon / Adhesive / General audience

055. Cava l'Alzinar / Eric Corretjé Zamora, Xavier Corretjé / Adhesive / General audience

056. Igrexario de Saiar, vino Albariño / Luis Carlos Galán Teijeiro / Adhesive / General audience

057. Tempranillo L'Alzinar / Eric Corretjé Zamora, Xavier Corretjé / Adhesive / General audience

058. Café Veracruz / Luis Carlos Galán Teijeiro / Rivet / General audience

059. Marqués de Gelida Gran Reserva Cava / Eric Corretjé Zamora, Xavier Corretjé / Adhesive / General audience

061. Natif Cava Brut Nature / Eric Corretjé Zamora / Adhesive / General audience

062. Leches especiales Kaiku / Perdinande Santxo / Adhesive / General audience

063. Binifadet / Jordi Duró Trouillet / Adhesive / General audience

064. Tierra de Cálogo, vino Albariño / Luis Carlos Galán Teijeiro / Adhesive / General audience

069. Azul y Garanza / David Alegria / Adhesive / General audience

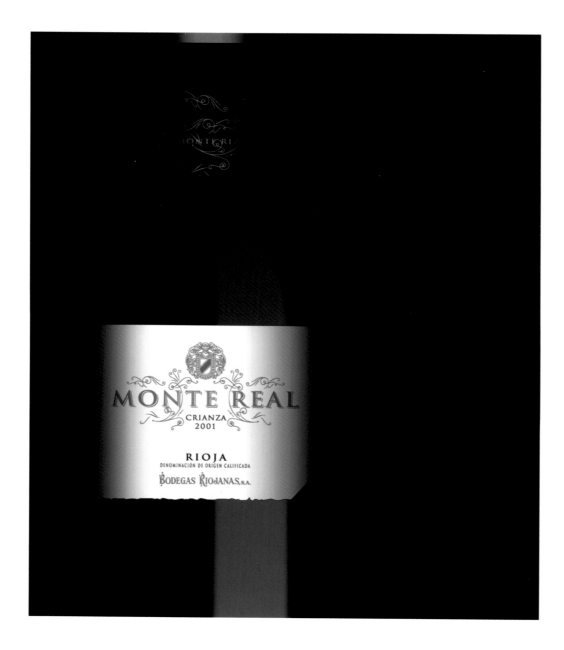

070. Monte Real Crianza / Natalia Tubía / Adhesive / General audience

071. Rosa de Azul y Garanza / David Alegria / Adhesive / General audience

072. Solagüen / Natalia Tubía / Adhesive / General audience

073. Seis de Azul y Garanza / David Alegria / Adhesive / General audience

074. Espirbel / Natalia Tubía / Adhesive / General audience

075. Bunrraty's Wines / Óscar Barroso Huertas / Adhesive / General audience

076. Viña Anzarena / Natalia Tubía / Adhesive / General audience

077. Palacio de Oriente / Pedro Alvarez / Adhesive / General audience

078. Aladro / Natalia Tubía / Adhesive / General audience

079. Cita del Sol / Pedro Alvarez / Adhesive / General audience

080. Casune / Natalia Tubía / Adhesive / General audience

085. Palacio de Sada / Pablo Recalde Equiza / Adhesive / General audience

087. Palacio de Sada / Pablo Recalde Equiza / Adhesive / General audience

088. Etiqueta de cerveza La Republicana / Eduardo Basterretche / General audience

089. Alcoholpop / Anita Repkes / Adhesive / General audience

090. Bodegas Luberri / Ramon Zumalabe - Doble Sentido / Adhesive / General audience

091. Nikolski Vodka / Anita Repkes / Adhesive / General audience

092. Vinos Camara / Salvador García-Ripoll / Adhesive / General audience

093. Perfektsoftdrink / Anita Repkes / Adhesive / General audience

094. Frised / Puigfalcó! / Adhesive / General audience

095. Torrent Fals, vino de crianza 2005 / Marilén Mayol / Adhesive / General audience

097. Lorenzo Quinn / Juan Linares / Adhesive / General audience

103. Nos Riqueza / Roberto Bacigalupe / Adhesive / General audience

104. Cantina Fratelli Pardi wine labels / Gianluigi Tobanelli / Adhesive / General audience

105. Celler Josep Ma Ferret Guasch / Simbiolisi - Albert G. Burzon / Others / General audience

106. Viejo Marchante / Pedro Alvarez / Adhesive / General audience

107. Irep / Natalia Tubía / Adhesive / General audience

115. Patatas Sedano / Monchi Pedreira Díaz / Others / General audience

116. Azeite Álamos / Pedro Albuquerque / Adhesive and Others / General audience

117. Fritravich / Eric Corretjé Zamora, Xavier Corretjé / Adhesive / General audience

118. Azeite Cartuxa / Pedro Albuquerque / Adhesive / General audience

119. Café Sorlidiscan / Eric Corretjé Zamora, Xavier Corretjé, Miguel Carreton / Adhesive / General audience

120. Azeite São Bruno / Pedro Albuquerque / Adhesive / General audience

122. Conservas Serrats / Gorcin Stanojlovic / Adhesive and Others / General audience

123. Puerros El Manojillo / Luis Sánchez Fernández / Others / General audience

124. Granjas del Marquesat / Ana Carnicer - cdroig / General audience

PUERROS: Aparte de las vitaminas A, C y de los elementos minerales, contiene sobre todo, aceites

INFORMACIÓN NUTRICIONAL POR 100 g

Valor energético	255/(61) KJ/(Kcal)	Vitamina A	10,0 mcg	Calcio	59 mg
Proteínas	1,5 g	Vitamina C	12,0 mg	Magnesio	28 mg
Hidratos de carbono	14,0 g	Vitamina E	0,9 mg	Fósforo	35 mg
Colesterol	0,0 mg	Niacina	0,4 mg	Potasio	180 mg
Fibra	1,8 g	Ácido Fólico	64,0 mcg	Sodio	20 mg

MUÑOZVAL

PUERROS
Producto Natural

Ctra. Serrada, s/n
47240 Valdestillas (Valladolid) España
Telf.: 983 55 10 17 / Fax: 983 55 11 61
www.centralhorticola.com

126. Mayava / Ana Carnicer - cdroig / General audience

127. Oretum / Pedro Alvarez / Adhesive, string / General audience

128. Aceites Soyfonsal / Ana Carnicer - cdroig / General audience

130. Aceites Terral / Daniel González Ferrer / Adhesive / General audience

131. Huevos Ecológicos / Pedro Alvarez / Others / General audience

132. Encurtidos Gourmet / Daniel González Ferrer / Adhesive / General audience

133. Ànima Dolça / Marilén Mayol / Adhesive / General audience

134. Especias Gourmet / Daniel González Ferrer / Adhesive / General audience

135. Packs Hit Nutrexpa / Jose Medina Cobo / Adhesive / General audience

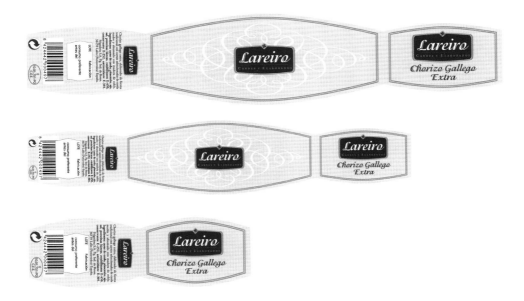

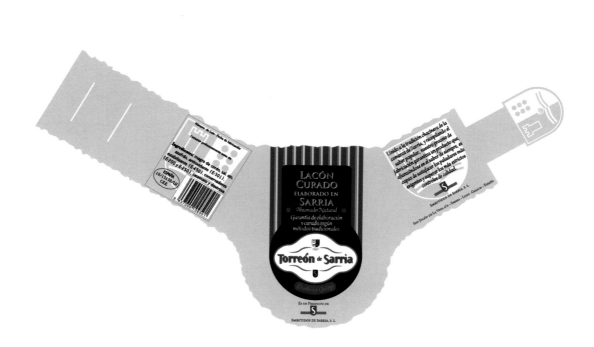

138. Torreón de Sarria / José Rivera / Adhesive and String / General audience

140. Algas Deshidratadas Porto-Muiños / Luis Carlos Galán Teijeiro / Others / General audience

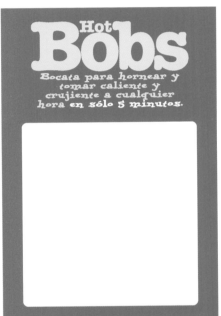

141. Bobs / José Rivera / Adhesive / General audience

142. Vinagre Vindaro / Natalia Tubía / Adhesive / General audience

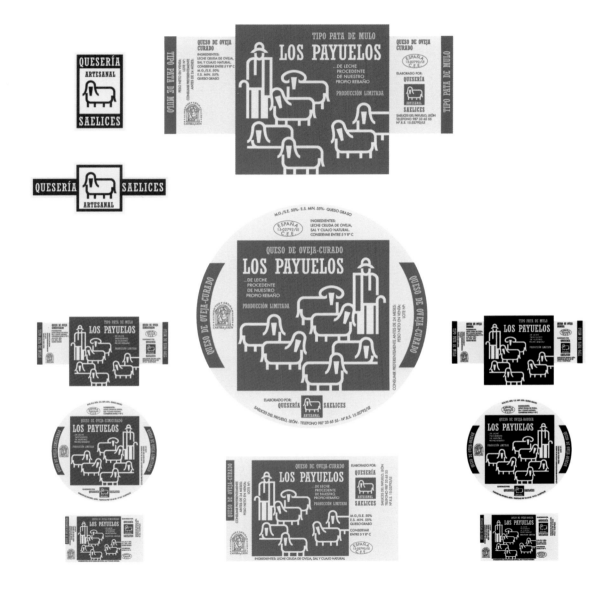

147. Quesería Artesanal Saelices / Santamarina Diseñadores / Adhesive / General audience

148. Clarici extra virgin olive oil label / Gianluigi Tobanelli / Adhesive / General audience

149. Borgovivo aromatic extra virgin olive oil labels / Gianluigi Tobanelli / Adhesive / General audience

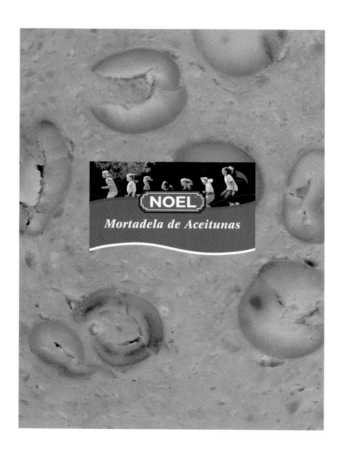

150. Noel, mortadela de aceitunas / Isidre Barnils / Adhesive / General audience

MISCELLANY

154. Christmas mailing - Strichpunkt 2000 / Melanie Schäfer / Adhesive / General audience

155. Agenda + Set Belleza Astor / Marc Mir / Others / General audience

156. Etiqueta Es Pot Vell para regalos artesanales / Luis Llabrés Manso / String / General audience

157. Dr. O'Meara, Pet Foods / D. Martijn Oostra / Adhesive / General audience

158. Floristería Pilar Casado / Álvaro González Pérez / Adhesive / General audience

159. Jabón Natural Eroski / La Machine / Others / General audience

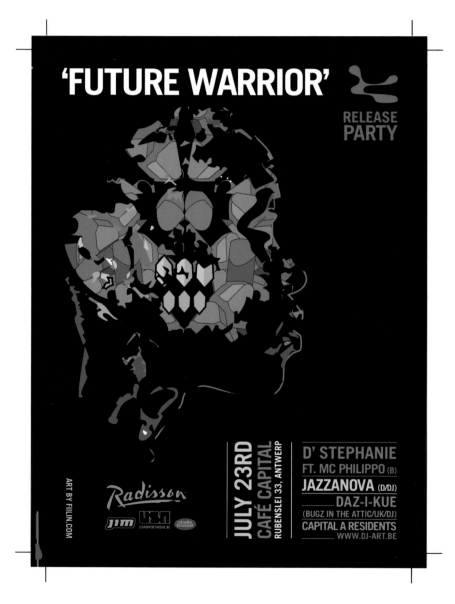

160. Flyer Sonar Kollktive / Juha Fiilin / Adhesive / General audience

165. Amoníaco Ferci / La Machine / Adhesive / General audience

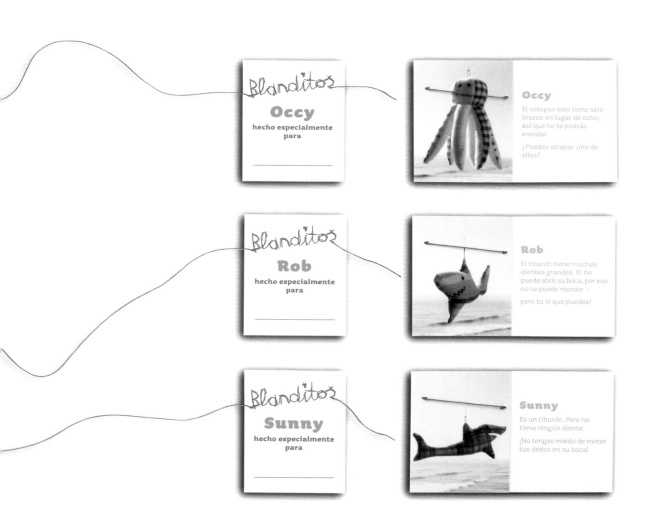

Blanditos
Occy
hecho especialmente
para

_____

Occy

El octopus solo tiene seis
brazos en lugar de ocho,
así que no te podrás
enredar.

¿Puedes atrapar uno de
ellos?

Blanditos
Rob
hecho especialmente
para

_____

Rob

El tiburón tiene muchos
dientes grandes. El no
puede abrir su boca, por eso
no te puede morder –

pero tu si que puedes!

Blanditos
Sunny
hecho especialmente
para

_____

Sunny

Es un tiburón. Pero no
tiene ningún diente.

¡No tengas miedo de meter
tus dedos en su boca!

167. With love / Emmi Salonen / Others / General audience

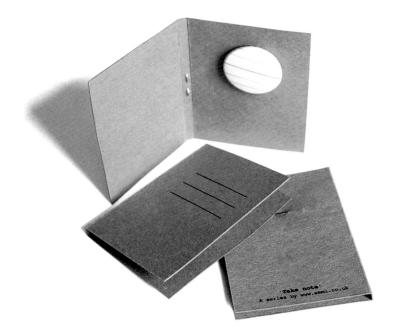

170. Home is... / Emmi Salonen / Others / General audience

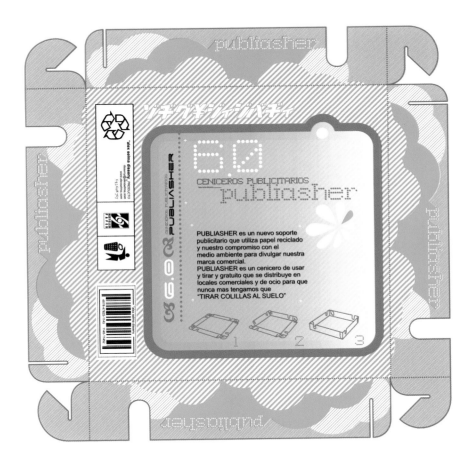

171. Publisher / Alex Selma Lázaro / Self-tied / General audience

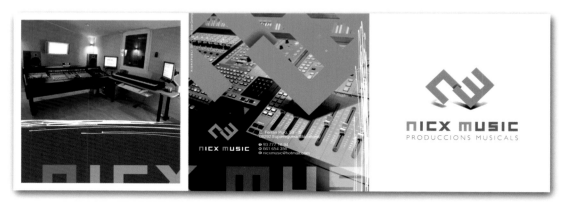

177. Hiroshi Watanabe - A tribute to Hiroshi Watanabe / (4976) mnp / Others / General audience

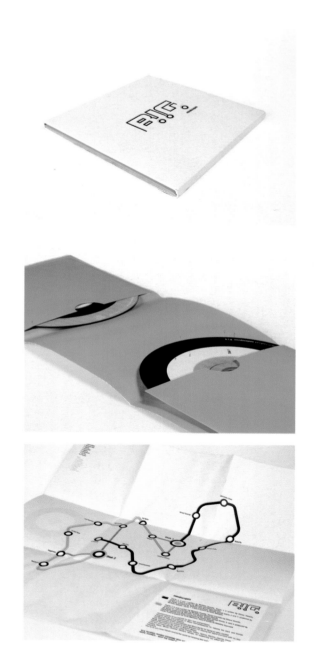

178. B.I.G mindscapes / (4976) mnp / Others / General audience

182. Mikael Delta - Dancing with an angel / (4976) mnp / Others / General audience

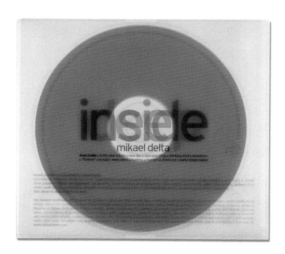

183. Mikael Delta - Deep Inside / (4976) mnp / Others / General audience

184. Mikro - 180° / (4976) mnp / Others / General audience

185. Mikos Diamantopoulos - 180° / (4976) mnp / Others / General audience

186. Tonqompilation / Caisten Raffel / Others / General audience

187. Tonqompilation / Caisten Raffel / Others / General audience

188. Xabier Colás / Others / General audience

189. G.PAL/1 / (4976) mnp / Others / General audience

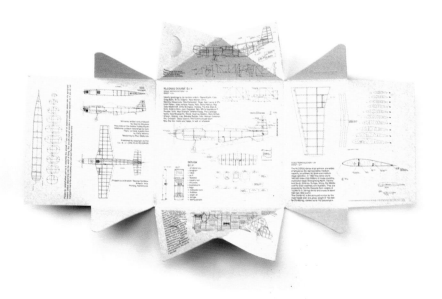

190. DOUSK D.I.Y / (4976) mnp / Others / General audience

191. Mermelada de lentejas / Estudi Regina Puig / Adhesive / General audience

192. Chris Nemmo - Forbidden Paths / (4976) mnp / Others / General audience

200. Etiquetas The Frederichoms Ownwear / Pep Valls / String / General audience

201. Electr / Estudi Clavé + Martín / Adhesive, string / General audience

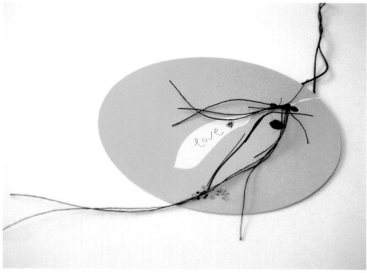

202. Girl Label T-Shirt. Thpplshp / Alex + María Cañada + Monferrer / String / General audience

203. Petralia Soprana / Estudi Clavé + Martín / Adhesive, string / General audience

204. The People Shop / Alex + María Cañada + Monferrer / String / General audience

205. Tan'am / Estudi Clavé + Martín / String / General audience

206. Baberos / La Machine / String / General audience

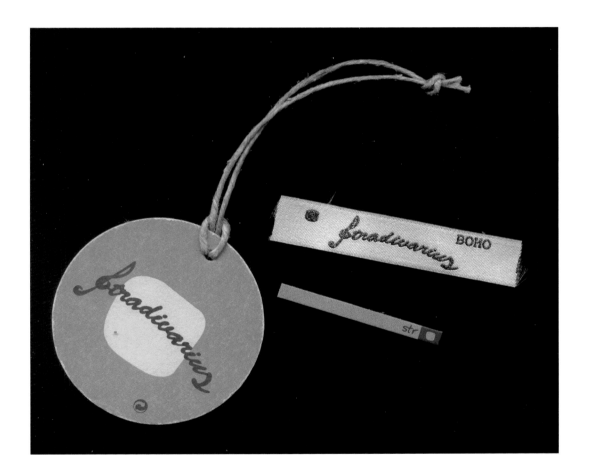

207. Stradivarius / Elena Serrano Campaña / Others / General audience

208. Silk / Paola Sinisterra / String / General audience

209. Enné, Diacar / Balcells - 3b Estudi / String / General audience

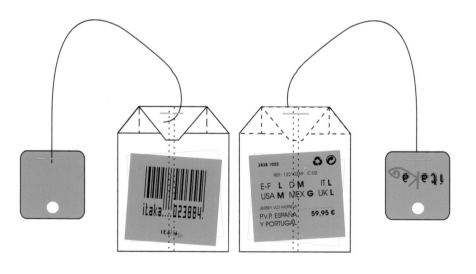

210. Itaka / Laura Clara Gallegos Braun / String / General audience

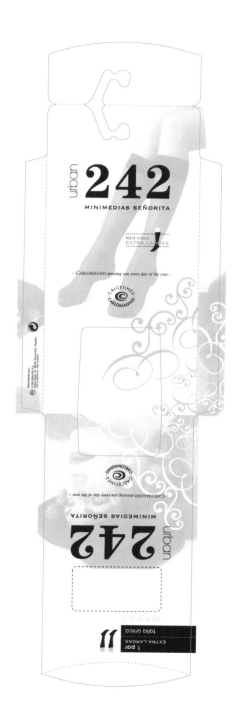

211. 242 Urban / Balcells - 3b Estudi / Others / General audience

TINTORERIA **LA RAPIDA**

212. Tintoreria La Rapida / Xosé Teiga / Self-tied / General audience

213. Cuattro, Tienda de Moda / Álvaro González Pérez / String / General audience

219. Fregona Sorli Discau / Eric Corretjé Zamora, Xavier Corretjé, Miguel Carreton / Others / General audience

CONTENTS

CONTENTS